The English Seaside

in Victorian and Edwardian Times

JOHN HANNAVY

Alum Bay and the Needles, c.1870. Idyllic views like this did a great deal to popularise the idea of a seaside holiday – offering the promise of a gentle unhurried lifestyle away from the bustle of the town.

SHIRE PUBLICATIONS

Published in 2011 by Shire Publications Ltd, Midland House, West Way, Botley, Oxford OX2 0PH, UK. (Website: www.shirebooks.co.uk)

Copyright © 2003 by John Hannavy. First published 2003; reprinted 2008 and 2011. Shire Library number 547. ISBN 978 0 74780 571 7.

John Hannavy is hereby identified as the author of this work in accordance with Section 77 of the Copyright, Designs and Patents Act 1988.

Printed in China through Worldprint Ltd.

10/1/3

British Library Cataloguing in Publication Data: Hannavy, John. The English seaside in Victorian and Edwardian times. – (History in camera; 14) 1. Seaside resorts – England – History – 19th century 2. Seaside resorts – England – History – 20th century 3. Seaside resorts – England – Pictorial works 4. Postcards – England – History 5. Outdoor photography – England – History 6. England – Social life and customs – 19th century 7. England – Social life and customs – 20th century I. Title 942'.081 ISBN 0 7478 0571 7.

Cover: *Clacton pier, 1896.*

Pictures that evoked seaside memories were not produced only by photographers based in the holiday resorts. While the image on the left was taken at Bridlington, the one on the right was taken by a studio in Warrington, several miles from the sea!

Contents

A group of travelling pierrots on an unidentified beach on England's east coast in August 1906. In the distance is a line of bathing machines with their attendant horses and handlers.

4

Acknowledgements

The images contained in this book were taken by a great many Victorian and Edwardian photographers – some well-known, others anonymous. Their work graced Victorian family albums throughout the land, and an even larger number of Edwardian postcard albums.

While the book contains many sepia images from 1860 onwards, and coloured postcards produced between 1902 and 1910, it is enriched by a rare and little-known collection of coloured photo-lithographic prints photographed and printed in the closing years of the nineteenth century by the Photochrome Company, originally from Zürich but with a London office from the mid 1890s.

No book is ever simply the work of the author, and this is no exception. My thanks, therefore, go to the many people throughout England who have answered my many questions – by letter, email and telephone – about the pictures and the locations. It is their knowledge of local history which has brought these images to life. With very few exceptions, the illustrations all come from my own collection. In many cases the originals have been digitally cleaned and enhanced to restore their quality. Thanks are due to Marilyn and David Parkinson, and to the many dealers and collectors who have brought exceptional and unusual images to my notice over the past thirty years. Thanks also to those readers who helped me identify the 'unidentified' pictures in the first printing.

John Hannavy, Great Cheverell, 2008

These 1/6th plate ambrotype images from the 1870s, taken in Yorkshire (left) and Dorset (right), were created by unknown travelling beach photographers. These unique direct-positive images on glass – the 'instant pictures' of their day – were processed inside the camera while the subjects waited.

Introduction

Photography and the seaside summer holiday grew up together. Both achieved huge popularity during the first half of the nineteenth century, and both enjoyed their heyday in the years before the First World War.

It is hardly surprising, therefore, that photography captured the magic of the Victorian and Edwardian seaside holiday in all its glory – from the simple beach portraits produced by the itinerant photographers of the 1850s, 1860s and 1870s, through to the sophisticated multicoloured lithographs which were sold in the 1890s as being 'real' colour photographs.

These 'Photochromes' are what you see on many of the pages of this volume, the direct predecessors of the colourful picture postcards with which we have all grown up. By the time the nineteenth century came to a close, photography was on the verge of becoming the popular hobby it has been ever since.

It would be quite wrong, however, to imply that the seaside holiday was a nineteenth-century invention. Enthusiasm for breathing the pure clear air of the seaside developed in the early eighteenth century, simultaneously at several points around the coast. Indeed, beach huts made their appearance in the early 1730s. Beach huts on wheels – forerunners of the ubiquitous

Ansteys Cove, Torquay, 1870s, a scene which changed very little in the following thirty years – see page 119.

Victorian bathing machine – appeared on Scarborough beach in North Yorkshire before 1735, while the bathing machine itself, the invention of one Benjamin Beale, first appeared on Margate beach around 1750.

1750 was a pivotal date in the development of the seaside holiday. Medical opinion at the time began to expound the therapeutic virtues of sea air, and of both bathing in and drinking seawater – taking the seaside 'cure'. For that idea, credit, if such it deserves, goes to several people, including Sir John Floyer and Dr Richard Russell, the latter of whom is also credited with being the primary moving force in the establishment of Brighton as a popular seaside resort. Public enthusiasm for the beneficial value of the seaside was spurred in the 1780s by its obvious endorsement by the Prince of Wales, later King George IV, who took up residence in Brighton.

Beale's original bathing machine was a much more elaborate idea than the one which appears in many of the beach scenes in this book. For example, it had a huge canvas hood which could be brought out to cover the area between the end of the machine and the surface of the water – allowing bathing in complete privacy. As one late-eighteenth-century guidebook explained, 'by the use of this very useful contrivance, both sexes may enjoy the renovating waters of the ocean, the one without any violation of public decency, the other safe from the gaze of idle or vulgar curiosity'. It is hard to relate such self-consciousness with a freely enjoyed holiday pastime. But the formality of the dress codes evident in so many of the pictures in this book – and they cover the period 1860 to 1910 – challenges whether or not the full pleasures of a relaxing seaside holiday could ever have been enjoyed by the participants.

Even bathing, apparently, had to conform to conventions and timetables!

In an August 1851 edition of his own magazine, *Household Words*, Charles Dickens wrote a delightfully perceptive essay on the seaside holiday, primarily about his home town of Broadstairs but

Enjoying the sun beneath the Alabaster Cliffs, Watchet, Somerset, summer 1862. This image is half of a stereoscopic ambrotype, an early three-dimensional picture, taken by local photographer James Date, whose studio was only a few hundred yards away. Nevertheless, because the plates had to be coated with their light-sensitive chemicals just before the picture was taken, and then developed immediately after exposure, Date would have had to take a portable darkroom tent with him and pitch it on the beach close to his camera.

applying to so many other expanding resorts. He wrote:

> So many children are brought down to our watering place that, when they are not out of doors, as they usually are in fine weather, it is wonderful where they are put; the whole village seeming much too small to hold them under cover. In the afternoons, you see no end of salt and sandy little boots drying on upper windowsills. At bathing time in the morning, the little bay re-echoes with every shrill variety of shriek and splash after which, if the weather be at all fresh, the sands teem with small blue mottled legs. The sands are the children's greatest resort. They cluster there, like ants: so busy burying their particular friends, and making castles with infinite labour which the next tide overthrows, that it is curious to consider how their play, to the music of the sea, foreshadows the reality of their after lives.

Undoubtedly, the major spur given to many of the emerging seaside resorts was the arrival of the railway. Railway development in the 1830s and 1840s was both rapid and extensive, and in the 1840s in particular the network of tracks linked most of the major towns, cities and resorts. That development continued into the 1860s and 1870s, bringing customers to the smaller and hitherto less accessible coastal towns.

The impact was enormous. When travel to and from the coast was restricted by the cost and limited availability of coach travel, a certain exclusivity was enjoyed by all those who made the journey to Broadstairs, to Brighton, or elsewhere. With cheap, fast and regular rail travel, all that changed. It is estimated that within a decade of the railway reaching Brighton, for example, the number of tourists visiting annually had multiplied thirty times to well over three million. For the middle classes, such a growth in tourism brought with it the disadvantage that the majority of the new visitors were 'excursionists' – working class families enjoying a day, or at most a few days, away from the monotony of their working lives.

Resort towns such as Clacton-on-Sea, Southport, and many others – which owed their existence entirely

A girl with her doll in an unidentified seaside resort, mid 1870s. Like so many early images, the photographer's name is unknown, as is his subject's. Beach photographers started to appear in the 1860s, often using ingenious cameras with ceramic interiors into which the coating and developing chemicals could be poured, removing the need for a portable darkroom tent. The photographer could prepare, take and develop a picture in a matter of minutes, before moving on to a different beach or even a different town.

to the growth in seaside holidays – expanded rapidly once the railway was built. For many other resorts, especially in the south-east of England, the introduction of steamer services to and from London offered an attractive and efficient alternative means of travel. And with the advent of the railway, and the potential increase in traffic, there was a parallel growth in the number of tourist beds available. Hotels proliferated, bringing much-needed employment to the locals.

The seaside holiday was enjoyed by all classes – statutory holidays were being introduced in the 1850s and 1860s – and some towns clearly catered for a more up-market clientele than others!

Despite the good times, and in true British fashion, hoteliers were always willing to grumble. Dickens made the following observation of Broadstairs in the 1850s.

> It must not be supposed that our watering-place is an empty place, deserted by all visitors except for a few staunch persons of approved fidelity. On the contrary, the chances are that if you came down here in August or September, you wouldn't find a house to lay your head in. As to finding either house or

Glimpses of the Blackpool sea front in the year before the Tower was built are relatively scarce and relatively small-scale. Both these carte-de-visite images were taken by local photographers Wolstenholme Brothers in 1879, when a severe storm did considerable damage to both promenade and pier only five years after the pier had been extended and completely renovated.

lodging of which you could reduce the terms, you could scarcely engage in a more hopeless pursuit. For all this, you are to observe that every season is the worst season ever known, and that the householding population of our watering place are ruined regularly every autumn.

The growing number of visitors to the resorts brought increasing demand for entertainment, once the novelty of walking along the promenade had been satisfied. Combining access to the resorts from the sea with yet another long walk, the seaside pier became commonplace.

The first of the major piers was opened at Ryde on the Isle of Wight in 1814, stretching 1200 feet (366 metres) from the promenade to the steamer. Before it opened, passengers to or from the mainland had had to be carried by porters from the boat to the beach.

It was a logical step, once the pier was established as an extension to the promenade, to encourage its use as an alternative bracing and invigorating walk. But when the railways brought the large influx of working-class visitors, the potential of the pier as a money-making enterprise started to be recognised. One of the first places to appreciate this possibility was Southport, in 1840, but it took the town another twenty years actually to construct its pier.

Once the idea of the pleasure pier had taken root – with charges set in place for promenading up and down it – it was a short step to the

The paddle-steamer 'Victoria' disembarks some passengers at Lulworth Cove, c.1906. With her sister ship 'Empress', this little steamer ran regularly to the cove from nearby Weymouth bringing day-trippers to one of the most beautiful parts of the Dorset coast. 'Victoria' had already been in service for over a quarter of a century when this picture was taken, and she did not go to the breaker's yard until the early 1950s.

development of the pavilion, housing a range of other attractions. The visitors were single-minded in their expectations – getting as close as they could to the sea, and having something to do while there. As *The Times* said in 1861, 'Down comes the excursion train with its thousands, some with a month's range, others tethered to a six hours limit, but all rushing with one impulse to the water's edge.'

Walking along Southport Pier in the 1860s cost 6d, unless, that is, you were embarking or disembarking from a steamer, in which case production of a ticket meant the fee was waived. Visitors and passengers using the 1200 yard (1097 metre) long pier, however, wanted something for their 6d. Complaints of the lack of seating to break up the long walk, of waiting rooms in which to shelter from the winds while awaiting the steamer, and of refreshment rooms, were all received by the pier company and acted upon immediately. Refreshment rooms were built on the pier, and a tramway was laid out to the pier head. One by one, the basic facilities of the pleasure pier were being put in place. Other pier companies dealt with like complaints in similar ways.

It was not until the 1880s and 1890s, however, that piers with great pleasure pavilions started to appear, often as replacements for earlier structures, and that pattern of replacement, extension and modernisation continued well into the twentieth century.

Just what sorts of images did the holiday-makers seek out as mementoes of their visit to Blackpool, Clacton, or any other resort?

Views of the beaches were the favourites in photography's early days, but they lacked the bustle and appeal of later images because of the limitations of the photographic process. Harbours were always popular, photographed at low tide so that the boats remained stationary while the picture was being taken!

Street scenes in the 'sepia' days were often described as depicting 'cities of the dead', being almost devoid of people, and populated only with a few stationary horse-drawn carriages.

As photography became more sophisticated, and the 'instantaneous' photograph became possible, the unpredictability – or perhaps the predictability – of British weather lent itself well to images of stormy seas crashing over piers and promenades.

This book provides a cross-section of the popular photographic prints and picture postcards which visitors to England's seaside towns bought in the period between 1860 and 1910. The fact that they have survived is testament to the fact that they were treasured by their buyers. Within a few years of the latest picture in this book being taken, Britain was at war, and life after that war would be very different. These pictures represent the last years of a soon-to-disappear lifestyle, captured by the photographers of Victorian and Edwardian England.

Early photography

Photography was invented in the 1840s – at about the same time that Thomas Cook introduced his first package holidays – and became a practical medium for photographing buildings in the 1850s. Because of the length of exposure, people in early photographs always had to be carefully posed. It was not until exposures shortened in the 1870s and 1880s that the casually observed holiday scene could be recorded by the camera.

Photography in its earliest days was a cumbersome process. Photographers had to make their own plates, coating large sheets of glass with the light-sensitive chemical emulsion just before exposure and processing them immediately afterwards. Not for them was the luxury of buying a box of plates and developing them at their leisure some hours or days later. This meant that, working on location, the photographer needed a portable darkroom close at hand in which to carry out all that chemical manipulation.

Sometimes this was a simple tent, which could be carried in a backpack, but for photographers such as Francis Frith, who toured the country taking thousands of tourist views in the 1860s and 1870s, a horse-drawn wooden carriage converted into a darkroom was the order of the day. For many, if not all, of the sepia location images in this book, such a facility would have been essential – with the photographer working in confined conditions inside a tent or a darkroom van, mixing ether with gun-cotton to create the 'collodion' mixture that carried the light-sensitive chemicals. The effects of prolonged exposure to ether fumes in such a confined space made early photography an unpleasant process to work with as well as a difficult one.

Flamborough Head, East Yorkshire, as seen by Carl Norman on a grey summer's day c.1870.

Commercially produced plates started to become readily available in the late 1870s, but huge cameras and large glass plates combined to require the carrying of a huge weight of equipment and materials to every location. Until the advent of enlargers with high-intensity light sources at the beginning of the twentieth century, most photographers made only contact prints from their work – the print being the same size as the negative. If a large print was needed, then so was a very large camera!

By the 1890s, when many of the coloured views in this book were taken, photographers still used large-format cameras but were able to capture their scenes with much shorter exposure times. Earlier views of seaside towns, streets and beaches seem empty, as only those few people who stood absolutely still during the long exposure were recorded on the glass plates. Others, who walked through the scene, stopping briefly for a second or two, appear as ghostly figures, half transparent.

Professional photographers continued to use large cameras up to the beginning of the First World War, and some even for some time afterwards, as it was easier to make contact prints from large negatives than to enlarge smaller ones. With the birth of amateur photography in the 1890s, however, and the proliferation of small hand-held cameras, amateur pictures started to take over from professionally produced ones. The sort of images visitors took home from their holidays moved slowly but surely from the professional images they could buy in print and book shops to the more intimate and informal mementoes they created themselves.

Before the 1890s, coloured photographic prints were tinted by hand, some photographic studios employing teams of women to do this painstaking work. All the coloured images in this book, however, have been artificially tinted at the publishing stage by the photographers and publishers who marketed them – real colour photography started to gain widespread popularity only as the period covered by this book drew to a close.

De La Warr Parade, Bexhill-on-Sea, 1905. The card was sent to Ulric from 'Nannie', who wrote that 'It is very hot here and we are all very brown, and I shall soon be like an old gipsy'.

Bexhill-on-Sea

Bexhill-on-Sea, situated to the west of Hastings, did not start to promote itself as a holiday resort until the 1880s, so these early postcards, produced in 1906, show that its popularity increased rapidly. Views taken as late as 1886 show a massive building site, with only a few houses completed and occupied. The development of the resort was the idea of Lord De La Warr, who owned the strip of coastal land and built fine terraces overlooking the sea. The resort was originally known either as Bexhill or Bexhill-on-Sea, to differentiate it from Old Bexhill, a short distance inland. The first motor race in Britain was held at Bexhill in 1902.

Blackpool and Lytham

The annual summer holiday in Blackpool invariably started with arrival at the 'excursion platforms' in Blackpool's Talbot Road station – later more blandly known as Blackpool North – seen here in 1903. At the time Blackpool had three stations. The eight excursion platforms were each capable of handling a nine-coach train, and at that time they were used only during the height of the summer season. For the remainder of the year, the main six-platform covered station was used. The main station closed in the 1970s, the present Blackpool North using only the former excursion platforms.

The coloured view of Blackpool Tower and beach, *c.*1896, on this page clearly demonstrates the popularity of the North-West's premier holiday resort in the closing years of the nineteenth century. All along the beach, almost hidden by the huge crowds, stalls selling everything from ice-cream to cheap gifts can be seen. Less than half a century earlier the town looked totally different. In 1840 there were only a few dozen houses along the sea front. The scale of the building programme in the second half of the century was remarkable.

Access improved considerably when the railway arrived in 1846, but it was only in the 1860s that the resort began to enjoy widespread popularity as a holiday destination – about the same time that Lancashire's workforce became entitled to statutory holidays.

The North Pier, the first of the town's three piers, was opened in 1863, and by the close of the century about three million visitors were coming to the town each year.

Blackpool's famous Tower – which took three years to build – was only two years old when this photograph was taken, having been completed in 1894. Modelled on Paris's Eiffel Tower, but at just over half the height, the 500 foot (152 metre) high tower celebrated Blackpool's pre-eminence as a holiday resort – despite the unpredictable weather of the North-West !

Blackpool's Talbot Square, in the town centre, always presented an animated and attractive scene to new visitors to the resort. In this picture-postcard view from 1905 there is not a car in sight. Horse-drawn carriages and the ubiquitous open-topped trams can be seen, but otherwise the streets are left to the pedestrians.

The Victoria Pier, now known as the South Pier, was opened in 1893, the third and originally the shortest of the resort's piers at a mere 430 feet (131 metres) in length. It was subsequently made considerably longer. It had shelters down its entire length and a magnificent pavilion. The pier has undergone extensive rebuilding since the 1950s as a result of serious fires.

Blackpool from the North Pier, a busy view taken in the early years of the twentieth century showing the giant Ferris wheel which was a feature of the resort for many years. The picture was taken c.1910 and published as one of the 'Pelham Sun Rays Post Card' series for Boots Cash Chemists.

Regent Terrace, number 163 in a series of carte-de-visite views of Lancashire and the Lake District published in the 1870s by the Manchester Photographic Company.

Blackpool's North Shore Promenade, seen from the Cliffs. This 1910 postcard demonstrates that, despite the crowds evident in other images of this ever-popular resort, it was still possible to find a relatively quiet corner.

The Imperial Hotel, Blackpool, from an 1870s carte-de-visite by Harold Petschler of Manchester, given to guests as both an advertisement and a memento.

A crowd gathers to watch those intrepid holiday-makers willing to risk all on the new water-chute – a forerunner of the huge Pleasure Beach that has become synonymous with the resort and is still a huge attraction today. Presumably, those racing down the chute towards the water were not dressed in their finery!

Central beach, Lytham, 1870s (top), taken by Francis Frith & Company. The contrast between the almost deserted beach and the bustle of Blackpool twenty or so years later (above) is remarkable. Only a few Lytham holiday-makers stood still enough to be recorded during the long exposure then necessary. The town started to develop as a holiday resort at the end of the eighteenth century, and despite Blackpool's proximity and popularity, Lytham retained its quietness.

Bognor Regis

Top: *Bognor beach, seen in a postcard from c.1905. Most of the bathers having returned to their bathing machines, they are being led back to the shore. Only a few hardy swimmers remain.*

Above: *This early-Edwardian postcard is not all it seems. It claims to show a storm at Bognor but is in fact a composite image – the storm is from one photograph, taken under very dull lighting, while the people are from another, taken on a bright, sunny day!*

The scene of bathing machines lined up along the shingle at the water's edge had probably been a part of Bognor's holiday routine long before the era of photography; indeed Bognor had adopted the bathing machine in the late eighteenth century. The town had first been recognised as a fine place to 'take the waters' in the 1780s, and by the mid 1860s had acquired a 1000 foot (305 metre) long pier and a reputation as a relaxing holiday venue.

Bournemouth

Above: *Francis Frith & Company took this view of a steamer at the pier from the East Cliff in the 1880s.*

Right: *Bournemouth from the West Cliff, published by James Valentine c.1906.*

Bournemouth had been a relatively quiet residential town until the arrival of the railway in 1870. It contained a mixture of high-quality villas on the steep slopes on either side of the River Bourne and on the cliffs overlooking the long sandy beaches. The easing of travel to and from the town changed that dramatically, and as the appeal of sea-bathing increased, so did the number of visitors arriving each summer. To cater for them, elegant hotels were built along the sea front, with others behind as the town expanded to meet the needs of a huge influx of holiday-makers.

Wide promenades, parks and tree-lined avenues met the needs of the rich but hardly catered for the new visitors. Initially the town offered little entertainment for them, but all that changed with the opening of the Winter Gardens Theatre in 1876 and the pier four years later.

Eugenius Birch's pier, originally just over 800 feet (244 metres) long, was extended twice – in 1894 and 1909 – finally reaching over 1000 feet (305 metres) into the sea, with a landing stage for pleasure boats at the head. Smaller craft were launched daily from one side of the pier, while bathing machines by the hundred lined the water's edge at the other side.

The East Cliff and Sands, seen from Bournemouth Pier in 1907.

Almost the same view, from a James Valentine postcard, a few years earlier. At this time the bathing machines were to be found to the west of the pier, leaving this beach to paddlers and sailors.

This animated view from the East Cliff looking down towards the entrance to the pier dates from c.1906. The pier had opened in 1880, bringing a dramatic increase in the town's popularity.

Bridlington

Below: *The New Spa, Bridlington, c.1905. A fairly late development – Scarborough further to the north was the more established spa – this group of late-Victorian buildings was dedicated to the idea that taking the waters brought great health benefits. The town did not offer the Edwardian tourist attractions of Scarborough, relying instead on its sheltered position and fine sands.*

Bottom: *Bridlington's Princes Parade, from a postcard sent on 15th July 1903. By this time the town had become a very popular resort and was attracting huge crowds of holiday-makers. The development of the sea front dates from the late 1860s, when the sea wall and promenade were created.*

Bridlington Harbour, seen here in the early years of the twentieth century, was a busy place indeed. In the foreground crowds are waiting to embark on a trip round the bay on the flotilla of small yachts, while in the middle distance the paddle-steamer *Frenchman* has just approached the quayside to take on board the huge crowds lining the harbour wall. This animated scene was photographed for Dundee postcard publisher James Valentine & Son.

The sailing craft took regular trips around the bay, and up to the spectacular Flamborough Head just to the north of the town.

Bridlington town was once known as Burlington, and at the time this picture was taken the area around the harbour was known as Bridlington Quay and was considered locally to have a quite separate identity. As the quay was the centre of the town's activity, the distinction was highly appropriate.

The harbour was also a thriving fishing port and, when not working, the fishing cobbles took tourists out on trips around the bay. A long-established part of the Bridlington holiday tradition was to gather on the harbour walls and watch the fishing fleet return and unload its catches.

The paddle-steamer *Frenchman*, registered in Hull, was built as a dual-purpose vessel. She had the power of a tugboat and the passenger-carrying capacity of a pleasure steamer. From the start of the 1899 summer season she returned to Bridlington every year and ran regular excursion trips along the North Yorkshire coast six days a week – never on Sundays. Built in South Shields in 1892 as the *Coquet*, she was renamed *Frenchman* in 1899 and thereafter served the town's holiday-makers each summer until she was scrapped in 1928.

It was quite common practice in many British ports at the time to reassign tugboats to excursion duty during the summer months. Such was the demand for these cruises that every possible space on the boat was taken up by tourists – even the open bridge, leaving the captain little space in which to control his vessel! Photographs survive of this vessel with several hundred passengers on board – and only two small lifeboats behind the funnel in case of disaster.

Brighton

The Electric Railway, seen here in 1904, was designed by Magnus Volk and opened in 1883, originally running from near the Aquarium to the Chain Pier. A few years before the Chain Pier was demolished, the line was extended to run underneath the pier and further along the beach.

Below: The holiday-maker's first sight of Brighton was its impressive station – seen here in early 1906 – a major terminus of the London, Brighton & South Coast Railway. The original 1841 station had been extensively rebuilt in 1883, at which time the impressive arched glass roof was added. In this picture a holiday train has just arrived and is about to disembark its passengers. A line of horse-drawn taxi carriages awaits them.

Brighton was the birthplace of the seaside holiday. When, in 1750, Dr Russell published his book about the health benefits of sea-bathing and the drinking of seawater, it was particularly the medical benefits of the waters at Brighthelmstone to which he referred. With its name shortened to Brighton, the town became the archetype of the English seaside holiday resort. Brighton and its waters were enjoyed from 1783 by the Prince of Wales, which did the town no harm at all.

In the nineteenth century the town was visited periodically by Charles Dickens, who often stayed at the Ship Inn in King's Road. While writing *Dombey and Son* in 1848 Dickens stayed at the Bedford Hotel and wrote the hotel into the narrative, with several characters staying there.

The London & Brighton Railway – later the London, Brighton & South Coast Railway – arrived in 1841, making a day trip to the seaside possible, and bringing Londoners in their tens of thousands. Between the 1840s and the end of the nineteenth century the town grew at a phenomenal rate to meet the ever-growing demands of the tourist trade.

The first of the town's piers – the famous Chain Pier – had opened as early as 1823 and served Brighton's holiday-makers for well over seventy years. The second – Eugenius Birch's West Pier – opened in 1866. With serious doubts over its safety, the Chain Pier was closed to the public in 1896 and, ironically, destroyed in a storm only a few months later. By that time its 'replacement', the wonderful Palace Pier, perhaps the most famous and beautiful pier in any of England's seaside resorts, was already under construction further along the beach and, after ten years of work, it was completed in its original design form in 1901.

Marine Parade and the Aquarium, c.1905. It is easy to overlook the impact of the motor vehicle, but in those days most of Brighton's holiday-makers arrived by train.

King's Road and the West Pier, 1904. This was Brighton's second pier, designed by Eugenius Birch, and often described as his finest. It was originally 1100 feet (335 metres) long, and completed in 1866. The pier head and its impressive pavilion were added during an extensive refurbishment in 1893.

On the Palace Pier, c.1908. The Palace Pavilion and Pier took ten years to complete. Opened in 1899 while still only partially built, its splendid pavilion was completed in 1901.

'Off on a Sail, by the West Pier, Brighton', c.1910. The yacht, owned by Fred Collins, laden with passengers, is about to set off for a pleasure cruise, while further along the beach the nearest bathing machine advertises 'mixed bathing'.

A group of Brighton's donkeys with three rather serious looking children on their backs, seen here on the Lower Esplanade adjacent to the King's Road, c.1910. Just behind the donkey-master, the ubiquitous bathing machines are as far up the beach as they possibly could be.

Broadstairs

The crowded sands at Broadstairs in the summer of 1908 at the height of the town's popularity as a seaside resort.

Broadstairs, as well as being a popular holiday resort, has more than a few literary connections. Charles Dickens, perhaps the town's most famous advocate – he regularly visited from 1836 until 1850 – wrote several of his most famous books while staying at various addresses in the area. Among the works created during his visits were *Pickwick Papers*, *Bleak House*, *The Old Curiosity Shop* and the closing chapters of *David Copperfield*. Today's town has several museums dedicated to the memory and legacy of the great man.

John Buchan wrote *The Thirty-Nine Steps* in 1914 while recovering in Broadstairs from an illness. The steps that inspired the title of his most famous thriller led down to the beach at the North Foreland.

Broadstairs is one of a group of resorts on the north-east tip of the Isle of Thanet. Broadstairs, like nearby Ramsgate, had no pier, and never developed many of the traditional features of the seaside resort. But with fine sands at the foot of the cliffs around Viking Bay, it still managed to attract many visitors each summer, despite the close proximity of Margate to the north.

The railway – in the form of the London Chatham & Dover Railway – arrived in 1863, bringing the expected benefits of easier access for holiday-makers.

In 1901, just a few years before these delightful images were taken, the town was linked with Margate and Ramsgate by means of the Isle of Thanet Electric Tramway.

Writing in 1850, Charles Dickens described a very different summer at

This view shows the continuing popularity of the bathing machine in the summer of 1905, with a tight line of them vying with tourists for what little beach was left uncovered by the sea at high tide. In Dickens's day, the town was renowned for 'excellent hotels, capital baths, warm and cold showers' and 'first-rate bathing machines'. Deck chairs were locally known at the time as 'lounge chairs'.

Broadstairs from the ones exemplified by the images on these pages:

> In the Autumn-time of the year, when the great metropolis is so much hotter, so much noisier, so much more dusty or so much more water-carted, so much more crowded, so much more disturbing and distracting in all respects, than it usually is, a quiet sea-beach becomes indeed a blessed spot. Half awake and half asleep, this idle morning in our sunny window on the edge of a chalk-cliff in the old-fashioned watering-place to which we are a faithful resorter, we feel a lazy inclination to sketch its picture.

He then went on to underline the tranquillity of Broadstairs, describing it as a quiet sleepy resort untroubled by the extensive developments taking place at other nearby seaside towns. He did acknowledge, however, that in July and August it invariably proved difficult to find a bed for the night. By 1863, when the railway arrived, his beloved town began to change out of all recognition. By the early years of the twentieth century, when these pictures were taken, Charles Dickens's opinion might have changed considerably.

Budleigh Salterton

Budleigh Salterton beach a few years after the opening of the railway to Exmouth. How little effect the line had made to visitor numbers! An unidentified paddle-steamer, run on to the shingle, is loading or unloading in the distance. In the foreground only six people can be seen – one for each of the bathing machines.

According to one late-Victorian tourist guide, Budleigh Salterton – close to the place where Sir Walter Raleigh was born in 1552 – had been 'spared the railway', so visitors to this quiet little resort at the end of the nineteenth century had to travel by coach or omnibus from the nearest station at Exmouth, 5 miles (8 km) away.

Budleigh Salterton was a favourite of the eminent Pre-Raphaelite painter Sir John Millais, who created his famous canvas *The Boyhood of Raleigh* there. Using as his models his two sons and a local sailor posed on the wall of the esplanade, Millais completed the painting in 1870.

To those who sought a quiet holiday, the fact that the village was all but cut off from the rest of the country meant fewer people, and more in the way of relaxation. It had started to enjoy some popularity at the beginning of the nineteenth century, long before railways influenced where people spent their leisure time.

Almost as soon as the ink had dried in the guidebook, the building of the Budleigh Salterton Railway was approved in 1894, opening as a single-track branch line connecting with Sidmouth Junction in 1897. By 1903 it had been extended to Exmouth, and the local businessmen who had sponsored its construction looked forward to the future prosperity that comes with larger numbers of tourists.

But the railway did not bring prosperity or an expansion of the tourist trade. Having a pebble beach rather than sands made it less attractive as a bathing place than the established resorts of Sidmouth and Exmouth to either side of it. Some visitors did arrive by one of the several paddle-steamers that plied the south Devon coast, but the lack of a jetty or pier made getting ashore a precarious undertaking, which sometimes involved getting one's feet wet!

Burnham-on-Sea

Burnham-on-Sea, a few miles south of Weston-super-Mare on Bridgwater Bay, owes its popularity as a holiday resort to the efforts of the Reverend David Davies in the early years of the nineteenth century. He envisaged the small town growing into a fashionable watering place and spa to rival Weston. Under his direction, a lighthouse was built on the beach to warn ships of the sandbanks, and the levies charged for this service were to be used to develop his spa.

Wells were sunk to raise water for the spa but, unfortunately, it tasted particularly appalling. The taste was not the only problem, apparently, and one contemporary commentator described the smell as being like a cesspit! So, while the resort enjoyed some success, the spa did not. The area, with enormous sand-dunes and safe beaches, was an ideal location for a holiday, and its popularity grew and endured for almost a century.

Despite being firmly in Great Western country, the railway that brought visitors to Burnham from 1874 was the Somerset & Dorset Joint Railway – and Burnham was the terminus of the line that ran north from Evercreech Junction.

In 1897, from the nearby Brean Down peninsula, the twenty-five-year-old Marchese Guglielmo Marconi sent a radio message across the 9 miles (14 km) to Lavernock Point on the Welsh coast – at the time the longest wireless transmission ever successfully carried out.

Children playing on Burnham beach, 1907. On the back of this card, Maggie, writing to her friend in Bath, described taking a paddle-steamer from Weston-super-Mare to Cardiff for the day – but saw fit to pass no other comment on either place.

Clacton-on-Sea

Clacton-on-Sea viewed from the offshore end of the pier, with the Waverley Hotel top left and the Royal Hotel, with its wide balconies, directly facing the pier entrance. A small steam launch can be seen tied up in the foreground. Considering the relatively short length of time the town had existed when this picture was taken, the sea front looks well established.

The entrance to Clacton Pier – known as the 'Gap' – seen in a late-Edwardian postcard.

The Promenade and Beach, Clacton-on-Sea, 1896. This view, looking towards the pier, is surprising for the number of soldiers in colourful dress uniforms who have been persuaded to pose for the camera.

The double-page spread overleaf shows Clacton Pier in 1896. Twenty-five years old when this photograph was taken, the pier had been built between 1870 and 1871, and extended and refurbished during 1890 to 1893. In this form it was really only three seasons old, and enjoying considerable popularity. Beyond the polygonal cast-iron pierhead pavilion was a landing stage for the steamers that sailed between the resort towns of the south-east. A twin-funnelled paddle-steamer, probably the *Koh-i-noor*, can be seen approaching the jetty at the end of the 1200 foot (366 metre) long pier. At the entrance to the pier, Belle Steamers advertise their service to Harwich, Gravesend and London. At the time, Belle Steamers operated five boats around the Thames Estuary – *Clacton Belle* being the first of the line, and appropriately named after the resort that had effectively been manufactured to exploit the growing popularity of the seaside holiday.

Clacton had been little more than a village before the pier was built. Steamer access and the arrival of the railways had been pivotal in putting the resort within easy travelling distance of London, with its millions of potential holiday-makers. The Sea Water Baths at the entrance to the pier were leased by the proprietor of the Royal Hotel on the Promenade. Originally built as the offices of the pier company, the timber-clad buildings had spent some time as the Pier Dining Rooms, before becoming the popular seawater baths. The pier was further extended in the 1920s.

The steamer 'Koh-i-noor', seen off Clacton in 1896, was the larger of two steamers that regularly called at Clacton – the other being the 'London Belle', considered to be a rather less opulent craft. The popularity of steamer cruises in the Thames estuary and around the south-east coast of England can be appreciated from the crowds thronging the steamer's decks in this remarkable photograph. These were the days before a health-and-safety conscious society enforced rigid loading limits on coastal vessels.

Built in 1892 by Fairfield Shipbuilders of Govan on the Clyde, the 'Koh-i-noor' was one of the fastest steamers of her day – with a top speed of over 19 knots – and certainly the most luxurious. Scottish-built ships were considered the best and most reliable, and rival Belle Steamers had all their vessels built by Denny Brothers of Dumbarton. The 'Koh-i-noor' had an eventful start to her life – a collision while on her delivery voyage required a new prow to be fitted back in Scotland.

With her sister ship the 'Royal Sovereign', 'Koh-i-noor' was the pride of the Victoria Steamboat Association's fleet, and boasted such luxuries as two bathrooms, a restaurant capable of seating two hundred passengers, a floating post office, a hairdressing salon, and a host of other innovative features.

With a gross weight of 884 tons, the 'Koh-i-noor' was the largest steamer in service on the Thames at the time of her launch and originally operated on the route from Old Swan Pier near London Bridge to Southend and Clacton-on-Sea.

For such a luxurious boat – built at a cost of £50,000 – she had a remarkably short working life. Withdrawn from service early in 1914 for a major boiler refit, the First World War intervened and she never steamed again. She was laid up in Govan for the duration of the war, and eventually taken to Morecambe on the Lancashire coast and broken up in 1919.

Cleethorpes

The Promenade and Slip, Cleethorpes, Lincolnshire, on a busy summer's day in 1905, photographed by Harrison Brothers of Lincoln. Refreshment and amusement stalls are set out on the beach, and, although not visible in this picture, Cleethorpes also had a popular 1200 foot (366 metre) long pier, opened in 1875.

Titled simply, and appropriately, 'A busy day at Cleethorpes', this view leaves no doubts about the popularity of the Lincolnshire resort.

Clovelly

The picturesque North Devon village and harbour at Clovelly have been photographed regularly almost since photography began. Francis Frith & Company took the 1870s view from high on the cliffs (right), while the coloured Photochrome views (above and overleaf) date from 1896.

Holiday-makers visiting Clovelly on one of the steamer services that served the North Devon coast sometimes had a challenging end to their journey. The paddle-steamers could not negotiate the small harbour, nor even the shallow waters near the beach, so visitors had to be ferried ashore in small rowing boats – and then 'walk the plank' in all their holiday finery to reach dry land. This lovely image was photographed in 1907 for a locally available postcard.

For much of the first half of the nineteenth century, Clovelly was visited by only a few tourists. It was a thriving herring-fishing port, and therefore no more than a working village, until restoration of the buildings drew attention to its picturesque charms. The harbour had been refurbished and extended in the 1820s.

Charles Kingsley lived in Clovelly as a boy, his father being the vicar of the village church in the 1830s, and the village is used in his book *Westward Ho!*. In the 1860s the novelists Wilkie Collins and Charles Dickens both visited Clovelly and in their jointly written story 'A Message from the Sea', published in Dickens's journal *Household Words* in 1861, they based their appropriately named village of 'Steepway' on it.

By the 1870s an ever-increasing number of tourists were being helped ashore for their brief visit to the village. Photographers were quick to capitalise on the sales potential the visitors provided, one of the first to do so being Francis Frith, who offered for sale sepia prints of the main street. Others followed suit, and by the late 1890s the Photochrome view (left) was a best-seller.

The needs of the tourists were catered for at the Red Lion Hotel, the New Inn, and tearooms up the steep hill. Gift shops sold local views and gifts.

The main street, officially known as the High Street but locally and more prosaically known as 'Up-a-long' and 'Down-a-long', is one of the steepest in England – just how steep can be sensed from the view down towards the harbour on page 43.

Cromer

'This is a fine place, but maybe rather quiet', wrote Graham to a friend in Essex in 1909, adding that 'we are enjoying ourselves enormously as you might expect, but it is rather annoying to have just settled ourselves on a lounge chair by the sea and have to jump up because of the rain, which is what we have had to do this summer'.

Despite having been a well-loved location for sea-bathing since the late eighteenth century, Cromer in Norfolk did not begin to enjoy real popularity as a holiday resort until late in the nineteenth century. Little more than a fishing port in 1790, some smart villas were built around the harbour for wealthy summer visitors, but a hundred years would pass before the town started to cater for mass tourism.

For the holiday-maker more interested in bathing, walking and relaxing than in amusements, the bracing climate of the Norfolk coast had long been considered ideal. It is even mentioned in Jane Austen's *Emma*, published in 1816, where we are told that 'Perry was a week at Cromer once, and he holds it to be the best of all the sea-bathing places'.

It was the opening of a direct railway link that made the area accessible to a much wider group of people. But in Cromer that did not happen until 1887. The pier was built between 1899 and 1901, and the esplanade just a few years earlier. Perhaps the steep climb back up from the beach was a deterrent, although in these views few seem put off by the prospect. In the 1890s large hotels were constructed overlooking the sea, built like grand French châteaux, and with names such as the Grand, the Metropole and the Hotel de Paris.

Cromer from the beach, photographed on a quiet summer's day c.1907. Only one horse is in action, pulling a bathing machine towards the water's edge, while a few fishermen are tending to their boats on the incoming tide.

Rough seas in Cromer, c.1910. A small group of people is demonstrating the enduring British fascination with the weather while, in the middle distance, Cromer's 500 foot (152 metre) long pier, completed only a few years earlier in 1901, is deserted.

Ladies' Bathing Place, Dawlish, Devon, 1908. For the demure ladies of Dawlish beach, splendid bathing machines bearing advertisements for Pear's Soap were available for hire. For those a little less well off, changing facilities were provided in the large building on stilts in the centre of the picture, while modesty was preserved between changing room and sea by little tents on wheels which ran up and down a track! Bathing was still segregated in the opening years of the twentieth century. Although not evident in this view, the railway ran just behind the changing-rooms building and in front of the colourful terrace immediately behind it.

Dawlish

Dawlish has been a popular holiday resort almost since sea-bathing became popular in the middle of the eighteenth century. Described in the *Gentleman's Magazine* in the 1890s as 'A bathing village where summer lingers and spring pays her earliest visits', the town was always considered a rather refined place to take the waters. The famous Dawlish sea wall, which runs between the beach on one side and the tracks and the town on the other, dates from the arrival of Brunel's broad-gauge single-track South Devon Railway in 1846. The railway brought with it an increase in summer visitors, and indeed traffic grew so quickly on the line that the track was doubled in the mid 1850s. The line was one of the last lengths of the Great Western Railway to be converted from broad gauge to standard gauge in 1892, and at that time a double track from Exeter merged into a single track just south of Dawlish station.

Jane Austen spent a holiday at Dawlish in 1802 and wove her experiences into *Sense and Sensibility*, published nine years later. A regular visitor to the town was Charles Dickens, and part of *Nicholas Nickleby* is set just outside the town.

A very different view of Dawlish from the one opposite, this 1903 photograph shows the 'Family Bathing Beach' alongside the railway tracks. It was published by Chapman & Company, stationers in the town, and shows very few families, and no sign of bathing!

Local bookseller and stationer F. P. Boone, with two shops in the Strand, published this postcard view of the sands in 1909. It was taken from the other end of the beach to that on the postcard opposite and shows the breakwater from which that view was photographed.

Dover's Admiralty Pier, c.1896, with several paddle-steamers tied up at the quay. The steamer on the left nearest to the camera appears to be about to leave. Admiralty Pier formed the western arm of Dover harbour and for many years was the point of departure not only for passenger steamers to France but also for the many coastal pleasure boats that served the resorts of south-east England.

Dover

Captain Matthew Webb, photographed by the London Stereoscopic Company in 1875, the year he became a celebrated professional swimmer. This carte-de-visite was published in celebration of his success at becoming the first person to swim across the English Channel. The twenty-seven-year-old Webb achieved his feat on 24th August 1875, covering the distance from Dover to Calais in a little under twenty-two hours. His achievement brought him fame and some financial success, drawing him to ever more hazardous exploits. The last of those, an attempt to swim the rapids and whirlpools at Niagara Falls on 24th July 1883, cost the Shropshire-born swimmer his life. This portrait of him remains familiar to millions, a stylised version of it having graced matchboxes for more than a century. A statue of Webb was erected on Dover's promenade in commemoration of his historic swim.

Dover's elegant Marine Parade, seen here in a picture-postcard view by Valentine of Dundee in 1910, with the Connaught Hotel nearest to the camera. Just behind the hotel the masts of a ship can be seen in the Western Dock. Today's busy cross-Channel ferry terminals are located to the east.

Eastbourne

Eugenius Birch, eminent pier designer and engineer of the 1860s, started work on Eastbourne Pier in 1866. It opened to the public in 1872, after almost six years of construction. Birch also designed piers at Blackpool, Bournemouth, Brighton, Deal, Margate, New Brighton and Weston-super-Mare. At over 1000 feet (305 metres) in length, Eastbourne Pier is said to be one of his finest achievements. This photograph was taken after extensive modifications and improvements carried out in 1901.

The railway reached Eastbourne in 1849, bringing the town within easy travelling distance of London, but the resort was barely able to give visitors a bed for the night! Photographs from the 1850s reveal a small seaside town that had seemingly spread in a haphazard manner along the coastline. All that changed with the development of the resort in the second half of the nineteenth century. The waterfront, with its 3 miles (5 km) of fine beaches, was redeveloped with fine villas, hotels and shops – the driving force was the Duke of Devonshire, whose name was given to the fine parks that were laid out at the same time. The result was a resort that catered for all tastes, offering everything from the typical seaside pier to elegant tree-lined promenades. The town took its reputation as a provider of the ideal holiday very seriously indeed, being proud to advertise not just the quality of its hotels, streets, shops and entertainment, but also its sanitary arrangements and the quality of its drinking water.

Eastbourne Parade and beach (above), seen in 1896, were the epitome of the genteel holiday resort. The beach is very little changed from the view (below) taken a quarter of a century earlier. Privacy while bathing was still expected by Eastbourne's visitors, although it would appear that most preferred to wait for the tide to come in before taking to the water. The elegant terraces of hotels and shops date largely from a massive redevelopment of this stretch of coastline during a twenty-year period in the middle of the nineteenth century. The main picture was produced by the Photochrome Company of Zürich, while the smaller image comes from Francis Frith's nationwide series of sepia views marketed in the 1870s.

This charming view of children playing on Eastbourne beach was probably taken in 1907 and was posted in the summer of 1908 to an address in Wallington, Surrey. According to the sender, that summer it had 'rained a lot, but not enough to stay in'.

Eastbourne from the Wish Tower, 1908. The Wish Tower was one of a series of Martello Towers erected along the south-east coast as a defence against possible Napoleonic invasion in the late eighteenth century. In total 103 towers were built from Aldeburgh in Suffolk to Seaford in Sussex. The photographer's vantage point for this picture, Tower No. 73, is now a museum.

Exmouth

This carte-de-visite view of Exmouth beach, taken by Francis Frith & Company in the early 1860s, is typical of the visual mementoes taken home by mid-Victorian holiday-makers. Reproduced here slightly larger than the original, these little photographs mounted on 10 cm by 6.5 cm (4 inch by 2½ inch) cards were designed to fit into the Victorian family portrait album. By the 1880s, Frith's photographic empire had been expanded to include every seaside town in Britain.

Almost half a century separates this 1908 postcard from the Frith image above, but Exmouth seems to have changed little. It was still the quiet Georgian resort it had been since the eighteenth century. A few of the Georgian houses still survive in 2003.

Filey

The rugged North Yorkshire coast between Bridlington and Scarborough has some of the most beautiful and dramatic coastal scenery in England. For holiday-makers, a visit to the rocky cliffs at Filey Brigg offered breathtaking views and impressive seas. Between Filey itself and the rocky headlands, fine sheltered beaches were in abundance, but the drama of the headland, away from the crowds, attracted walkers and photographers alike. The photograph reproduced here, by Carl Norman, dates from the 1870s. To get this spectacular view, the photographer carried a huge plate camera taking a 15 inch by 12 inch negative out to the point. These were the days before it was possible to enlarge photographs, so if a large print was needed a large camera had to be used!

An additional challenge was the process used. The wet collodion process employed at the time required the photographer to coat his own plates and develop them immediately after he had taken the picture. So he needed to carry with him all his processing chemicals, and a portable dark-tent in which to prepare and process his plates.

Fleetwood

Passengers waiting for the ferry to Knott-End-on-Sea and Preesall across the river Wyre, c.1905. Before 1847 Fleetwood had been developing considerable ferry traffic with Scotland. The town marked the northern end of the railway line from London, and before there was a line across the border, travellers to Scotland sailed from Fleetwood to Ardrossan on the Clyde coast. Plans to develop the town as a major port never materialised after the railway to Scotland was opened. However, the town did enjoy considerable popularity as a holiday resort.

Fleetwood beach on a busy summer's day, 1910.

Folkestone

A solitary gentleman looks out over Folkestone Harbour in 1908. Beyond him two steamers lie tied up at the quayside. A popular ferry port for the crossing to France since mid-Victorian times, Folkestone started to develop as a seaside resort when the railway was opened in the 1840s.

Folkestone from the Leas, 1907. On the edge of the beach, tucked hard in against the cliffs, an amazing wooden helter-skelter – predecessor of the roller-coaster – can be seen just below the pier. It must have been a white-knuckle ride when the tide was high. The pier, long since demolished, was completed in 1888.

Travelling entertainers were a popular feature of the Edwardian seaside holiday, sometimes performing in marquees or makeshift platforms on the sands, and at other times enjoying the luxuries of a pier pavilion, a bandstand or an open-air theatre. Here a group of pierrots performs on a sunny summer's day on Folkestone's East Beach in 1910.

At under 700 feet (213 metres) long, the Victoria Pier, built 1887–8, was of modest proportions. Beyond the pier pavilion a floating landing-stage had been added two years after the pier opened. This view dates from 1904. A fire in 1945 closed the structure and it was demolished in 1954.

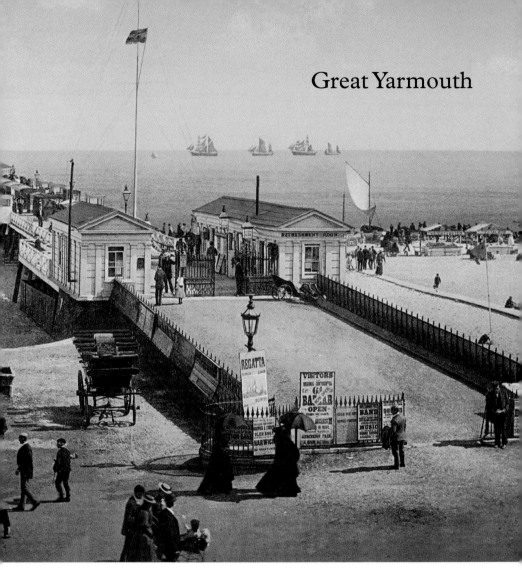

Great Yarmouth

Great Yarmouth's original Britannia Pier, 1896. The seaside pier acted as a magnet for visitors to many resorts, offering entertainment, promenades, gift shops and a host of other amusements. Rival attractions, such as Wright's Noted Tea Bar, grew up on the sands alongside, offering a host of other ways of parting the holiday-makers from their money. On this pier, the attractions included the Original Continental 6d Bazaar, brass-band concerts, an aquarium, and even a photographic studio adjacent to the Refreshment Room. From the end of the pier visitors could embark on steamer trips on the 'Glen Rosa' to Harwich and London. Five years after this picture was taken, the forty-year-old pier was demolished to be replaced by an 800 foot (244 metre) structure.

Souvenir, fish and grocery stalls on Great Yarmouth promenade, with the jetty or south pier beyond, photographed c.1896. This remarkable view ably illustrates the attractions of the late Victorian seaside holiday. The busy jetty, the stalls along the promenade, and the considerable number of yachts and other vessels offshore all testify to the success and popularity of the seaside holiday, and of Great Yarmouth as a resort in particular.

The revolving tower was a feature of several English resorts, although the idea originated in Atlantic City in the United States of America. Great Yarmouth's was the first in England, opened in 1897, and was located adjacent to the entrance to the Britannia Pier. Five years later the company which had built the structure had gone bankrupt, and it was sold to a local business consortium for £2000. It survived until 1922. Revolving towers could also be found at Douglas, Morecambe and Scarborough. Others were planned for Margate and Southend. The idea had been patented in 1894 and involved a passenger platform that was raised and rotated by electricity generated from a steam engine at the base. Counterweights eased the loading on the engine.

Great Yarmouth's New Britannia Pier, completed in 1902, replaced the pier seen on page 61. The pavilion, by local engineers Boulton & Paul of Norwich, was later replaced by amusement arcades.

The East Cliff, Hastings, 1896. This end of the beach was often quiet, the crowds preferring the miles of sand to the west. Fishermen have hauled their boats up on to the shingle here for centuries. In 1900 the town had a fishing population of almost three thousand men and rising. This area, known as the Stade, also housed all the support industries – and the group of tall, narrow wooden buildings at the top of the shingle beach housed chandlers, net lofts and other crafts that helped maintain the fleet. The net lofts were built high on foundations only 8 feet (2.4 metres) square to minimise ground rent!

Hastings

> There, amid the little shops and the little libraries, bath-chairs and the German bands, the Parade and the long Pier, with a mild climate, and a moderate scale of prices, and the consciousness of a high civilisation, I should enjoy a seclusion which would have nothing primitive or crude.

Thus Henry James, the American-born Victorian novelist and one of several famous writers to live in the town or visit it, described Hastings in 1883 as the ideal place to retire to.

The town's 900 foot (274 metre) long pier was opened in 1872, complete with covered walkways – despite the town's claim to have a gentle climate – and a fine pavilion capable of seating two thousand people. The famous Eugenius Birch had had a hand in its design, as he had with many other piers in the South-east.

Bathing was a popular pastime in Hastings from the beginning of the nineteenth century and remained strictly segregated for over a century; until well into the twentieth century a low breakwater on the bathing beach separated the sexes. On the west side, the striped bathing machines were clearly labelled 'gentlemen', while those on the east were labelled 'ladies'. Both lines of bathing machines screened the bathers from the crowds on the beach and nearby Carlisle Parade. Amazingly for a town that depended for centuries on the fishing industry, Hastings never had a harbour, and several grand schemes to create one were started but never completed. The last major such project was in the early 1890s, when one arm of a new harbour was built. It still survived in 2003.

Yachts starting, Hastings. In this 1896 view, Hastings Pier can be seen through the sails of the leading yacht, while an animated group of holiday-makers looks on. Beyond the pier, miles of fine sandy beaches stretch towards St Leonards and Bexhill. Hastings Pier was built to a Eugenius Birch design and opened in 1872. It reached just over 900 feet (274 metres) into the sea.

The sea front, the pier and Carlisle Parade, Hastings, photographed by the local Gower studio c.1900. There is no sign of any motor vehicles – only horse-drawn carriages and a single tram in the middle distance. Entrance to the baths – seen above the bathing huts – cost 6d. E. G. Hutchinson's bathing machines line the beach nearest to the camera.

Built between 1869 and 1872, Eugenius Birch's Hastings Pier started off life as a typical Victorian pier, with a wide, open promenade and a theatre at the pierhead. Later, covered walkways were added, and after a fire in 1917 a new theatre was built. A century after the pier opened it offered two theatres, a zoo and amusement arcades. Admission to the theatre cost between 6d and half a crown in 1910. In this postcard the colourist has accidentally removed the funnels from the paddle-steamer.

Hastings, in a storm in 1906. This postcard was sent as a New Year greeting to a friend in Watford in early January 1907. It would appear that most resorts offered unseasonal as well as seasonal views to their postcard-buying public. Elsewhere in this book similar stormy views at Bognor Regis and Blackpool offer vivid contrasts to the idyllic holiday beaches crowded with tourists. 'The sea is just like this today', wrote Nellie from Hastings to her friend Mrs Irving. Such an image seems dramatically at odds with Henry James's comment that one of the town's major attractions was that it enjoyed 'a mild climate'.

Carlisle Parade and Robertson Terrace, Hastings, 1905. This photograph, taken from a favourite viewpoint for photographers, presents an untypical scene – a crowded promenade, but an almost empty beach behind the wall of bathing machines at the water's edge. In the distance two yachts are preparing to take holiday-makers out for a sail. By the time this photograph was taken the segregated labels had been removed from the bathing machines, but it is believed that there was still segregation.

Herne Bay

The beach, Herne Bay, seen from the Clock Tower, photographed in 1910. It is clear from such images that many beaches were more than just for the benefit of the tourists. The boat tied up at the water's edge appears to be loaded with timber.

The Clock Tower, Herne Bay, was built in 1837. At the time the town, formerly a fishing village, was being redeveloped as a holiday resort. By the end of the nineteenth century the 1873 pier had been extended in length to just under 4000 feet (1219 metres), making it one of the longest in the country. Just out of view, a splendid pavilion was being built at the time of this 1908 picture.

Hove

Hove beach, 1910, with shingle rather than golden sands, was less attractive as a holiday destination and much quieter and more sedate than its neighbour Brighton. It had no pier to attract visitors to the sea front, which instead was lined with elegant villas and apartment buildings. On this stretch of the beach, mixed bathing was permitted.

Queen's Parade, Hove, seen here in a postcard from 1909, together with nearby Grand Avenue exemplified the elegance of the town in Victorian and Edwardian times.

Hythe

Top: *Hythe beach and esplanade, 1907, displaying all the attributes of a popular holiday resort – bathing machines, donkeys, model yachts and full-size fishing boats – but without the crowds. Hythe, in Edwardian times, was said to prefer the more genteel holiday-maker – the one who eschewed the razzle-dazzle of the pier and seaside entertainments, preferring instead the quiet coastal walk. With shingle beaches rather than sand, Hythe never attracted large crowds of visitors.*

Bottom: *The promenade, Hythe, 1909. 'It is a lovely place', wrote May to her friend in Hull, adding that the highlight of her stay so far had been a walk to Saltwood Castle, a Norman ruin to the north-east of the old town. Hythe itself was set back somewhat from the sea, the seaside resort being separated from the town itself by the nineteenth-century Royal Military Canal.*

Ilfracombe

Top: *A paddle-steamer entering Ilfracombe harbour in 1909. Ilfracombe became, for a time, the most popular holiday destination on the North Devon coast. As with so many other towns, it was the arrival of the railway – in this case a branch line from Barnstaple in 1874 – which initiated a period of growth. By the end of the nineteenth century grand hotels and guest-houses had been built, and the population of the town had doubled to meet the needs of the influx of holiday-makers.*

Bottom: *The paddle-steamer 'Britannia' seen here en route from Weston-super-Mare to Ilfracombe in the early years of the twentieth century, heavily laden with holiday-makers. She was built at the McKnight yard in Ayr and entered service linking the harbours and piers of the Bristol Channel in 1896. The record for the fastest journey from Weston to Ilfracombe is still held by this vessel. Later rebuilt with twin funnels and a bigger boiler, she continued in service until the mid 1950s.*

Isle of Man

Douglas beach, at the height of the 1896 summer season, catered for a different class of bathers at each end. In this view, the simple pleasures of paddling in the sea, skirt tucked into knickers, is being enjoyed by children close to the camera, while the more refined approach to taking the waters – away from prying eyes – was being discretely catered for in the privacy of the bathing machines further along. On the hilltop above the promenade, the Falcon Cliff Hotel and Pleasure Ground included a Grand Pavilion designed in the style of a miniature Crystal Palace. Not long after this picture was taken the hotel was sold and the pavilion demolished.

Photographers quite often set up 'outdoor' backdrops to create an all-weather solution to the seaside photograph (such as the rigging used in one of the first pictures in this book) – all the appearance of the outdoor life without the discomfort! But why did photographic studios in the Isle of Man make so many of their customers sit in pretend boats?

Frederick Woodcock of Douglas Head Road took this 'outdoor' shot in the 1870s. He styled himself as 'Artist in Photography' and as being 'Patronised by Prince Leopold, Duke of Albany'. One wonders if he made the Duke sit in the boat as well...

Frederick Johnson had his studio in the same road as Woodcock but had a bigger boat in it! His could cater for four friends at a time.

Most ambitious of them all was Henry W. Moore who, on his cartes-de-visite, styled himself as 'artist and photographer' with studios in Castle Mona Road 'near Wallace's Baths'. He had the biggest boat of them all, the splendid eight-seater seen here!

On the south-west tip of the Isle of Man, Castle Rushen, seen here in 1896, remained a haven of peace well away from the tourist centres of the island's east coast. The Norman fortress adjacent to the little harbour was a magnet for photographers then as today. It has had a colourful history, including partial destruction in the fourteenth century at the hands of the Scottish king Robert the Bruce. Having been used at various times as both a prison and a lunatic asylum, the castle has undergone numerous alterations and subsequent restorations since the seventeenth century. A major restoration a few years after this picture was taken removed many of the Victorian additions.

Isle of Wight

Cottages and boats
near Shanklin
(above),
photographed in
1896.

(Left)
Paddle steamer
arriving at Ryde
Pier, c.1902. The
boat is probably
the 443 ton PS
Duchess of Fife,
built in Clydebank
in 1899, which
regularly served
the route between
Southsea and
Ryde. The
postcard was
produced by Paris-
based publisher
Louis Levy.

Ryde Pier in 1910 with a steam train making its way up the track to the pierhead. This pier comprises three separate structures side by side – one each for railway, tramway and pedestrians. At 2250 feet (686 metres) in length, it is the longest of the eight piers that once graced the Isle of Wight – and the pedestrian pier is also the earliest, having been built in its original form in 1814, over sixty years before Yarmouth Pier (overleaf) and seventy-five years before Shanklin Pier. Ryde Pier was rebuilt several times during its lifetime, most significantly in 1859. Ryde's other pier – the Victoria Pier, construction of which was started in the 1860s but never completed to its original grand design – was demolished in the 1920s. The island's other surviving piers are at Sandown, Shanklin, Totland Bay, Ventnor and Yarmouth. The eighth, Cowes Pier, built in 1902, was demolished in 1951.

Freshwater Bay, photographed by Poulton of Ryde in the early 1870s. Not far from this beach scene stands Dimbola Lodge, home at the time of the great Victorian photographer Julia Margaret Cameron. Nearby was the home of Alfred, Lord Tennyson.

Land's End

The attraction of Land's End goes back a long way, and the place has drawn photographers almost since the invention of the camera. One of the first professional photographers to market commercial images of the rugged westernmost point in England was Penzance-based professional Robert H. Preston, who took the images seen here in the early 1870s. The views were mounted on to standard-sized cartes-de-visite, designed to be displayed in the Victorian family album.

Wolf Rock Lighthouse. This 'instantaneous' picture was taken from the deck of the steamer 'Solva', which had been specially made available to the photographer by Trinity House. At the time the picture was taken, the lighthouse had just been completed after ten years of construction in a most inhospitable location. Work on the stack had commenced only months after the last in a long line of shipping disasters. As Preston wrote, 'no heavier or more terrific seas are to be found than sweep over it'. The tower rose to a height of 116 feet (35 metres), with walls between 7 feet and 9 feet (213 cm and 274 cm) thick. It was constructed on a stepped base, the steps intended to help break the force of the waves. In all, nearly 4000 tons of granite was used in its construction, using dovetail joints to lock the blocks together as further protection.

Land's End itself, from Preston's 'Royal Series of Cornish Views', c.1875. In those days visitors could enjoy the views of the dramatic 200 foot (61 metre) high cliffs free of charge. Today well over a million people a year pay for the privilege.

Littlehampton

Set between Bognor Regis and Worthing, Littlehampton's life has revolved around its harbour since the Middle Ages. It enjoyed some success as a holiday resort from the early nineteenth century, with its fine beaches and lush parklands between the town and the sea. Well-known for its sandy beaches and dunes, it offered safe bathing everywhere except near the harbour (below) and the fast-flowing estuary of the river Arun. In the middle of the century it was considered a quiet place for a holiday – one contemporary guidebook accused it of being perhaps too quiet – but by the time these pictures were taken in the early years of the twentieth century it was quite busy during the summer months. Unlike its neighbours either side it never acquired a pier, and that surely contributed significantly to the sense of peace on the promenade (bottom).

Lowestoft

On the morning of a yacht race at Lowestoft in 1909, a small steam launch makes its way among the yachts as they prepare for the competition. Through a gap in the sails, a large steamer can be seen tied up at the jetty. At the time this picture was taken, Lowestoft was enjoying considerable popularity as a resort but was primarily a busy fishing port, with over seven hundred boats working from its harbour.

The beach and Claremont Pier, Lowestoft, photographed c.1906, only three years after the pier was completed – the fifth from last pier to be built in England. Unusually, given the date of its construction, the 750 foot (229 metre) long pier was originally built of timber, and at that time it was a simple open affair, principally designed for steamer access. A pavilion was added a few years later.

Lynmouth

Left: *The Lynton & Lynmouth Cliff Railway, which linked Lynton at the top of the 500 foot (152 metre) high cliff with Lynmouth at the foot, used gravity to raise and lower the cars. The weight was provided by huge water tanks beneath the passenger cars. It was completed in 1890, thanks to a great deal of money from the eminent publisher and philanthropist George Newnes, some fifteen years before this view was taken. The 900 foot (274 metre) long track climbs a gradient steeper than 1:3 and is still going strong well over a century after it was built.*

Below: *At the foot of the cliff, Lynmouth, photographed in 1896 by the Photochrome Company, was a peaceful village much loved by those seeking a quiet holiday.*

Margate

This view of Cliftonville, Margate, photographed in 1910 on a busy summer afternoon, epitomises the Edwardian era, with the fine clothes of the holiday-makers, and their relaxed and confident demeanours.

In the world of the seaside resort, Margate's great claim to fame is having been the birthplace of the bathing machine – that ubiquitous hut-on-wheels which preserved the modesty of middle-class Victorians. Benjamin Beale is claimed to have invented the machine in 1753, and by the time the pictures on these pages were taken, the town had welcomed holiday-

Margate Harbour, from a postcard sent by a visitor in 1907, with Eugenius Birch's pier beyond. The pier, a relatively early one and Birch's first design, was opened in 1856. By the time this picture was taken the pier had been considerably extended and enlarged no fewer than three times.

A paddle-steamer, probably the 'Koh-i-Noor', approaching the jetty at the end of Margate Pier in 1906. As well as being Birch's earliest creation, this was the first pier to use the patented screw piles that became the mainstays of many subsequent designs. The octagonal pierhead that the steamer is approaching was completed in 1878.

makers for over a century and a half. Always one of the livelier resorts in south-east England – and certainly offering more entertainment than its near neighbours Ramsgate and Broadstairs – Margate offered several beautiful bathing beaches stretching between its two more subdued suburbs, Westgate-on-Sea in the west and Cliftonville in the east.

The Govan-built 'Royal Sovereign', leaving Margate in the summer of 1904 on her return journey to Tilbury. The Royal Sovereign was the sister ship to the 'Koh-i-noor' (see Clacton-on-Sea), although she was slightly different in appearance, her forward funnel being slightly further forward than the Koh-i-noor's. Built by Fairfield Shipbuilders, she was a few tons lighter than her sister and spent much of her working life on the Tilbury to Margate route. In order to get her under some of the Thames bridges the upper section of her funnels could be retracted – hence the strange funnel shape. She entered service in 1893 and was withdrawn in 1929.

Morecambe

Above: *Morecambe's donkeys pose for the camera, c.1910.*

Left: *The Promenade near the Winter Gardens, 1907. Yacht trips around the bay are being advertised by the Victoria Sailing Company.*

Opposite page: *Trains bringing holiday-makers to the Lancashire resort of Morecambe, just as at Blackpool, arrived at specially designated 'excursion' platforms at Morecambe station. Morecambe was nothing more than a group of villages before the railway was built. The line was built between 1846 and 1848 and, once open, the town grew rapidly. This view dates from 1906.*

A line of horse-drawn omnibuses waiting for passengers at the entrance to Morecambe's West End Pier (above), c.1908. The pier was completed in 1896 and extended 1800 feet (549 metres) into Morecambe Bay, with a fine pavilion just under half-way along. By 1917 the pavilion had been destroyed by fire and, after severe storm damage, the length was reduced by half in 1927. It was the town's second pier – the first, Central Pier (below), having been opened twenty-five years earlier. It was just over half the length of the West Pier. The children bathing were photographed c.1909.

Mortehoe

This 1896 view of the Barricane Shell Beach near Mortehoe in North Devon contains everything needed for a seaside holiday – sea, sand, donkeys and a cuppa! With only nine people on the beach, the staff of Parker's Tea & Luncheon Tent seem ready to serve tea to

rather more people than we can see. With its beautiful views, this area was popular with photographers – and a photographer can be seen lying beside his vintage plate camera and tripod.

New Brighton

New Brighton Tower in the Wirral resort of the same name was built by the same company which built Blackpool's tower a few years earlier. It was completed in 1900 after almost three years of construction work and, at over 620 feet (189 metres), was 120 feet (37 metres) taller than Blackpool Tower. Despite its popularity with tourists from across the Mersey in Liverpool, it stood for only twenty-one years before being dismantled. The ballroom and entertainment complex at its base was open for another forty years, until it was destroyed by a catastrophic fire in the late 1960s.

New Brighton was conceived and constructed as a fine holiday resort for the people of Cheshire – 'a favourite and fine watering place' was how the proposed town was described in the planning prospectus. There was not even a village there before Liverpool entrepreneur James Atherton bought a huge tract of the Wirral peninsula with the specific intention of developing the resort in the 1830s. His vision was of fine hotels and fine villas on a series of terraces rising from the water's edge and overlooking the beach.

The houses were to be designed so that those on one level did not obscure the sea view afforded to the houses behind. Atherton envisaged steamer services linking the resort with Liverpool. Sadly it was not to be. Fifteen years after work started there had been little success in realising Atherton's grand plans. The fine hotels and the grand terraces never materialised, and only a few of the planned elegant villas were built – although extensive residential streets were actually laid out. Atherton's plans for the steamer services to Liverpool did come to fruition, however. The resort eventually did develop – but as a southern alternative to Blackpool, even down to the tower, catering not for holiday-makers but for summer day-trippers from Liverpool, across the Mersey.

New Brighton Pier, 1907. Eugenius Birch designed the only pier on the Wirral peninsula for the New Brighton Pier Company and it opened in 1867. It took less than two years to build – by Manchester engineers J. & A. Mayoh – and had a unique observation tower that afforded fine views of the Mersey estuary, then one of the busiest waterways in Britain. It also served as the ferry-boat terminal bringing visitors from Liverpool. Safety concerns closed the pier in the 1960s.

The beach and the Higher and Lower Parades, seen in 1908, with an assortment of hotels, tea rooms and dining rooms lining the sea front. The building of the container terminal at Seaforth in the mid twentieth century caused current changes, which swept away most of the sands!

Landing mackerel, Newlyn, Cornwall, 1909. This animated scene was once typical of many small Cornish fishing ports, but Newlyn is one of very few that kept its fleet throughout the twentieth century. A few years before this picture was taken the port was the scene of riots, as fishermen made their feelings known about their east-coast rivals fishing on the sabbath day.

Newlyn

Newquay

Newquay beach, in a postcard mailed in 1907, offering us a view that had changed very little in the thirty years since the town had reinvented itself from a working port into a holiday resort. This postcard, like so many others before the outbreak of the First World War, was printed in Saxony – where colour printing seems to have been at a much more highly developed state than in Britain.

A quiet fishing port with a considerable pilchard fishing fleet until the arrival of the railway, Newquay quickly became a popular destination for Victorian holiday-makers. In less than twenty-five years the town's population trebled to meet the needs of the increasing numbers of tourists. It takes its name from the New Quay, built in the middle of the fifteenth century and funded by the then Bishop of Exeter. Newquay was ideally suited for a holiday. Sheltered beaches with safe bathing appealed to the needs of the Victorian bather. One late-nineteenth-century guidebook noted that it was sheltered from the prevailing winds, had extensive flat beaches, and sands firm enough for tennis to be played on them. Another guidebook suggested that while the town was popular in summer, it was more dramatic in autumn and winter when huge waves crashed ashore. Those waves are, today, the town's passport to success as a surfer's paradise. They must have posed quite a challenge to the Victorian bather stepping demurely down from the bathing machine

The railway arrived late in Newquay – a branch line was laid in 1875 from the Great Western Railway at Par Junction to the east – and was not originally conceived as a passenger line. It was one of a number of mineral lines laid to the small ports of Somerset, Devon and Cornwall, in this case to carry china clay down to the busy harbour. The railway's impact on the town, however, was dramatic, and resulted in a considerable number of hotels being built in the following decades.

Paignton

Top: *Paignton's bathing beach, seen here in 1910 in a view taken from the pier. Like so many other places, it was no more than a quiet village until the railway arrived in the mid nineteenth century. In the 1870s, this was a favourite holiday haunt for the inventor of the sewing machine – Isaac Singer – and nearby Goodrington Sands is still a popular seaside venue today.*

Bottom: *The Esplanade and Paignton Pier, taken at about the same time. The pier was completed in 1879, one of only three built on the south Devon coast. Of the others, only one still survives – at Teignmouth. Paignton's bathing machines were operated by the Paignton Bathing Company, whose large multiple-bathing machine can be seen on the beach just below the pier.*

A quiet corner of Ramsgate's Royal Harbour, seen in an 1896 print. The harbour was given its 'Royal' title after George IV's 1822 landing there, and a monument to the event stands on the East Pier. Extensive redevelopment of the area in the nineteenth century resulted in the construction of elegant terraces around the north side, and of the New Road – running between the harbour and the terraced street above.

Ramsgate

Ramsgate sands in summer, with the pier beyond, seen in a postcard published in the early years of the twentieth century. At the bottom right of the picture a beach photographer's camera can be seen set up and ready for use. Ramsgate Pier was built in the late 1870s, to a length of 550 feet (168 metres), but had a short life. Damaged twice during the First World War, once by collision and once by a mine, it was eventually demolished in 1930.

This 1905 photograph is titled 'Koh-i-noor making Ramsgate Harbour' and the paddle-steamer looks every bit as crowded as it does in the Clacton-on-Sea pictures earlier in this book. By this stage of the steamer's career, she had been moved to the Tilbury–Margate service, sharing the route with 'Southend Belle'. They were by then known as the 'husbands' boats' – used by men working in London during the week and returning to their Kent and Essex families and homes at the weekend. To wives and children, the steamer approaching Ramsgate Harbour on a Saturday afternoon was a welcome sight indeed.

Ramsgate, facing due south across Sandwich Bay, offered a slightly busier location for a holiday than quiet Broadstairs to the north, together with less wind and a milder, more sheltered, climate. Its busy harbour and quiet beach to the north-east offered variety to the visitor. Like many other large resorts, the town operated electric tramways, with open-topped cars. The journey down the steep incline to the harbour must have been exhilarating at times, testing the brakes on the vehicles to the limit. In the worst of the weather the upper deck would have been an unpopular place to sit, but on a sunny day like this it offered tourists the chance of an open-air ride around the town. On the front of the tram on the right is an advertisement for locally made Kennard's Kentish Jams. The photographer's vantage point, looking over the town towards the west, offered a fine view of the busy Royal Harbour and the grand terraces of shops above.

The postcard was posted to the sender's father in St Albans in August 1905 by a holiday-maker who was splitting her time between Ramsgate – where she stayed at Beaconsfield House – and the more bustling resort of Margate to the north.

Redcar

The Esplanade, Redcar, looking east. The Esplanade and the new sea wall, seen here in a 1905 view, do not present the ideal image of the thriving holiday resort. A single sweets or ice-cream stall sits on the edge of the almost empty beach close to the camera, while a few others – sadly not enjoying a healthy trade – can be seen in the distance. A glimpse of the pier can also be seen at the far left of the picture. The Redcar Pier Company was formed in 1866, but no start was made with construction for over five years until, allegedly spurred on by a similar project in nearby Coatham, the company pressed ahead. The pier opened in 1873 after an expenditure of over £6000. At 1300 feet (396 metres) in length, but with only a ticket office and an open promenade deck, it enjoyed only a few trouble-free years before being cut in two by a ship in 1880. That collision cost over £1000 to put right! Two further collisions in 1885 and 1897 and a catastrophic fire in 1898 added to the company's woes. Only a fragment of the pier survives today.

The postcard was produced by Raphael Tuck, whose company has been at the forefront of postcard and greetings-card production in Britain for well over a century. How times have changed – the card is postmarked 10 p.m. on 21st February 1905, with a second postmark stamped Paddington at 9 a.m. the following day!

Redcar, a few miles south of the mouth of the Tees, was a successful holiday resort from the early years of the nineteenth century, its 10 miles (16 km) of sandy beaches being a particular attraction as sea-bathing became widely fashionable. When the tide went out, it went out over a mile!

In late-Victorian and Edwardian times, the town itself largely consisted of a single street running parallel with the coast, many of the houses facing away from the sea. The railway arrived in the mid 1840s, offering a direct link with Middlesbrough, hugely increasing the number of visitors to the resort. The line continued round the coast linking the town with Saltburn-by-the-Sea.

There was never the huge development that took place at resorts further south, and despite its undoubted popularity, Edwardian Redcar was best suited to holiday-makers who created their own amusements. Today's town with its sea-front amusement arcades is very different.

St Anne's-on-Sea

St Anne's Pier on the Lancashire coast was built in 1885, and the pavilion seen here was completed in 1904, the year before this picture was taken.

St Anne's was also the site of a camp built especially to give a seaside holiday to Manchester's underprivileged children. This 1903 card shows 'dinner time' with the children, wearing the required camp uniform, gathered together for their midday meal.

St Ives

Above: *Quay Road, St Ives, c.1910. In the middle of the nineteenth century, this was the largest pilchard-fishing port in Cornwall, with a large fleet of boats operating from the eighteenth-century harbour. At the same time it was growing rapidly as a holiday destination. A mixture of quaint old houses and narrow streets, Edwardian St Ives celebrated its unique architecture in picture postcards.*

Left: *The Pictorial Stationery Company produced a series of 'character' postcards in the period of 1908–12, depicting local people, costumes and customs – almost as an ethnographic study of a foreign race! While pictures of women gutting fish, fishermen mending nets and men building fishing boats were obvious subjects, this tableau of a boy with a milk jug and a girl with a broom was a somewhat more unexpected one.*

Scarborough

Scarborough beach and harbour from Francis Frith's series, 1870s.

Right: *Thomas Harrison had a camera and mobile darkroom set up on the beach in the 1860s when he produced this fine ambrotype glass positive image of a horseman.*

If the popularity of any Victorian or Edwardian holiday resort can be gauged by the number of photographic images available for visitors to take home with them, then the popularity of Scarborough was beyond dispute. From the earliest days of the medium, photographers were available to cater for all tourist tastes.

The spa town at the beginning of the twentieth century had come a long

From the mid 1860s, this stereoscopic view of Scarborough's South Cliff is from a series of three-dimensional images which could be viewed in the drawing-room stereo viewer. It was photographed and published by George Washington Wilson of Aberdeen.

Above: *At Scarborough harbour, fish girls at work mending nets regularly drew crowds in the early 1900s.*

Below: *A carte-de-visite view of Scarborough Castle, c.1870, by local photographer George Willis.*

way from its humble beginnings 250 years earlier. When sea-bathing was first promoted along this coast in the seventeenth century, it was not for the modest or faint-hearted.

At that time there was nothing like the protective enclosure of the bathing machine while changing followed by the shielded descent into the water – a naked immersion was considered to be by far the most efficacious approach! Scarborough's spring waters had first been discovered in the early seventeenth century, and their 'medicinal' value was immediately promoted.

Dr Wittie, a local physician, first advocated the combined therapy of drinking the bitter-tasting waters from the spring and bathing in the sea as early as 1660. Sea-bathing became popular about a hundred years later, and this probably marks Scarborough out as the first seaside resort in England.

The spa buildings were completed in 1880, close in to the cliffs on the South Bay, and their terraces afforded fine views of the sea.

Scarborough Spa and Promenade, as seen in a postcard from 1908. A few years earlier, Scarborough had been described as the 'Queen of English watering-places, spread out like an amphitheatre upon a bay'.

Scarborough harbour also drew amateur photographers, keen to create their own memories of their visit. The early years of the twentieth century were marked by the introduction of the Kodak camera and the birth of amateur photography as a mass hobby. This gentle, romantic view was taken by photographer Harry Wanless in the summer of 1906 and published in 'Focus', a popular photographic magazine of the day.

Sidmouth

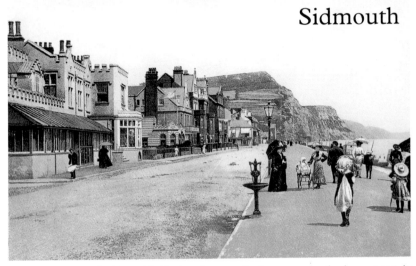

This 1905 view of Sidmouth's Esplanade suggests it was never the busy resort its developers planned it to be. In the late eighteenth century it was described as 'tolerably frequented in the bathing season'.

The oldest picture postcard in this book, this crudely printed composite series of views of Sidmouth was sent to an address in Somerset on 15th July 1901. Until January 1902, messages could be written only on the picture side of the card. Only the address was permitted on the other side. A Queen Victoria halfpenny stamp was used, despite the fact that the Queen had died earlier that same year.

Skegness

A group of golfers on Skegness Golf Links in 1910 playing a course that is a far cry from the manicured greens and fairways of today.

Skegness beach, also about 1910, with horses saddled up and ready to be hired to visitors. Just in front of the stables, children are being led past on the ubiquitous seaside donkeys.

Even today, the lifeboat is always guaranteed to bring out the crowds at any holiday resort. Here the Skegness lifeboat, with its fourteen-man crew, is being launched from the beach in front of a huge crowd of onlookers. The design of the 1800 foot (549 metre) long pier, completed in 1881, was selected from a competition entry of over forty designers.

Southampton

Southampton Water offered both residents and visitors an opportunity to see the great ships of the world. The huge transatlantic passenger ships shared the seascape with the British fleet. Ever since photography was capable of recording their presence, photographers have turned their cameras towards these impressive vessels.

Below: HMS 'Orlando' at anchor in Southampton Water in 1860. George Washington Wilson of Aberdeen marketed many views of the great ships of the day.

Bottom: Isambard Kingdom Brunel's mighty 'Great Eastern' and an accompanying tugboat in Southampton Water, 1860, also photographed by Wilson. This huge vessel, six times the size of anything built before, marked the genesis of large passenger ships. Despite her opulence and size, she was a commercial failure and spent much of her life as a cable-laying ship.

Southend-on-Sea

Below: *The West Parade, Southend-on-Sea, as it looked in 1896. By this time the town was often referred to as 'Whitechapel-on-Sea' as railway access made it an ideal day-trip for visitors from London. The railway arrived not long after the pier was completed, and brought an enormous influx of holiday-makers. Benjamin Disraeli lived in Southend in the 1830s, but he would not have recognised the town had he returned once its reputation as a resort had become established.*

Left: *Southend Pier is acclaimed as the longest in the world. Work started on the 1800 foot (549 metre) long pier (pictured in 1896) in July 1825 and was completed by 1830. By the mid 1840s it had been extended to over 7000 feet – almost 2 km! That was to bankrupt the pier's owners, and the part-finished project was sold in 1846 for the sum of £17,000. Further extensions ensured that it retained a deep-water jetty, and there was room for three large steamers to tie up all at the same time!*

To cope with the fluctuations of the tide, the pierhead allowed ships to load or unload at three different levels. A rebuild in the 1880s replaced the ageing wooden structure with iron supports, and that is basically what survives today. Work started on the new pier in 1887, and it was officially opened three years later. The public had been allowed access the year before, without the benefit of the railway to take them to the pierhead. Yet another extension to the pierhead in the late 1890s – to maintain the depth of water, which had reduced as a result of silting in the Thames – took Southend Pier to its record-breaking length of just over 7900 feet (2.2 km). The electric railway – essential given the length – enabled passengers disembarking from the steamers to ride in comfort to dry land. This 1896 view, looking back from the pavilion towards the town, dates from just before work started on that last extension. The electric railway was built at a lower level than the promenade deck – along the right-hand side of the pier as seen in the view on the left.

In the twentieth century the pier was further extended to give it a length of 7874 feet (2.4 km).

In 1896, when this view of the Cart Parade in Southend was taken, the resort was enjoying considerable popularity yet a number of the buildings along the front still seem to be private residences. Among them, however, and eager for the tourist's shilling, the Rose Coffee Tavern was ideally positioned almost opposite the end of the jetty nearest to the camera. A further three crowded jetties can be seen in the picture. Further along the parade, the Hope Commercial Hotel, the Palace Hotel and a number of others all offered visitors the ideal seaside view.

The Cart Parade seemed aptly named, for behind the crowds of tourists the roadway is lined with carts and carriages.

Southport

A horse-drawn tram makes its way down Lord Street in the 1890s.

The resort of Southport, a few miles along the Lancashire coast from Blackpool, has always offered a much less brash holiday experience than its northern neighbour. Southport's popularity as a holiday resort dates from the late eighteenth century, although, more accurately, it was the village of Churchtown which pioneered the idea – Southport itself was the name given to the resort in the decades that followed. The elegant streets and arcades that typify today's town were developed during the 1820s and 1830s, and by the middle of the nineteenth century the town was attracting huge crowds of holiday-makers. To service their needs, Southport's population grew from one hundred at the beginning of the nineteenth century to ten thousand by the 1860s. Built just a little too close to the mouth of the River Ribble, Southport has forever suffered from the build-up of sand and silt from the estuary – a problem that has consistently increased the length of the walk to the sea. In the 1840s and 1850s, however, when the town started to enjoy considerable popularity, the tide regularly came close in to the sea front. Plans for a pier were first proposed in the 1840s, with ideas of developing the town as a commercial port, but by the time the pier opened twenty years later it was clear that the future lay in the development of holiday attractions. To ensure that there was pleasure-steamer access at all stages of the tide, the pier had to extend 1200 feet (366 metres) out over the huge expanse of sand!

Coconut shies and an assortment of souvenir and food stalls line Southport sands c.1875.

High tide in the late 1860s, with the Royal Hotel in the middle distance.

With miles of sand and frequent strong winds, sand-yachting was popular in the 1860s.

Southsea

South Parade Pier in 1904, on a dull and quiet day. A plume of smoke from a departing paddle-steamer can be seen at the end of the pier, but few holiday-makers are in sight. South Parade Pier was originally constructed in 1878–9 and was extensively damaged by fire not long after this picture was taken. Little of the pier seen in this view survived that fire. The rebuilding was completed in 1908 and much of the surviving pier dates from that period of rebuilding.

Clarence Esplanade, on a fine summer's day in 1905, with every summer entertainment in evidence – swimming, sailing, fishing, promenading and the gentle pastime of just sitting reading in the sunshine.

Much of the holiday activity in Southsea was to be found around the South Parade Pier and the adjacent beach, but to the south-west of the town was the much shorter Clarence Pier, adjacent to Clarence Parade. It was more a jetty than a pier in the established sense. For those wishing to bathe, bathing machines were available further along the shingle, behind the point from which this view was taken. Boating from the shingle was highly popular. From the other side of the pier paddle-steamers regularly made the short crossing to the Isle of Wight.

Southsea Castle, seen in a postcard view from 1906, was built by Henry VIII. Although just a few minutes' walk away from the bustle of the resort, this view presents a quiet impression of the seaside resort, which is today part of the city of Portsmouth.

Swanage

Swanage's famous globe was erected in the 1890s at Durlston Castle, a popular restaurant at Durlston Head a mile south of the town, giving holiday-makers a geography lesson while they promenaded. The town became highly popular as a holiday destination in the mid nineteenth century. In the 1880s, as ever with the arrival of the railway, large-scale development took place to meet the needs of a growing summer population.

Bathing in Swanage Bay, seen here in 1905, was in the hands of two local enterprises, White's and Silvester's, who between them owned all the bathing facilities. Silvester's Bathing Tents – which ranged from small tents on wheels to conventional bathing machines – catered for the more affluent, while White's Bathing Saloons offered cubicle changing facilities in the larger vehicles at the water's edge.

Teignmouth

Teignmouth Bathing Beach, 1907, complete with bathing machines advertising 'Pears Soap for your Complexion'. Teignmouth is unusual in having sands that are darker and redder than most nearby coastal resorts. Unusually for a postcard view, the photographer, from his vantage point on the pier, has chosen to point his camera into the sun, creating an unusually dark and sombre scene.

The Den Promenade, Teignmouth, 1910, with the pier in the background. Teignmouth Pier was completed in its original form as early as 1867 but was extended twenty years later. A new pavilion at the sea end was completed in 1890. Despite the huge popularity of the area with holiday-makers, Paignton, Plymouth and Teignmouth were the only South Devon towns to have piers. Plymouth Pier was demolished in the 1950s.

Torquay

From 'Frith's Series' of British views, this photograph of Torquay town and harbour dates from the late 1870s. The view is looking across the harbour towards Victoria Parade, completed in the early 1830s. The harbour was designed by eminent engineer and canal builder James Rennie, who completed the original walls in 1803. The outer breakwater was completed sixty years later, and the Promenade Pier in the 1890s. In what was always a working harbour, small pleasure-craft compete for space with commercial ships. Redevelopment in the 1960s has dramatically changed this view.

Torquay was notably described by Alfred, Lord Tennyson as 'the loveliest sea village in England', although by the time he first visited the resort it was already a small town. Thanks to its sheltered position at the north-western corner of Tor Bay, Torquay has long been renowned for its mild climate, and it was already a popular winter resort before the summer seaside holiday became universally popular in the mid nineteenth century. That popularity – from about 1790 – shaped the town's development, with elegant villas and terraces being built around the harbour, itself a creation of the early nineteenth century.

Brunel's Great Western Railway reached the town in the late 1840s and parts of Torre station date from that time, although the station was considerably enlarged in the 1880s. Torquay's original 1859 Great Western Railway station had been considerably outgrown by the 1870s, when a new station was built. The railway was originally constructed to Brunel's 7 foot gauge, and standard-gauge track was not laid until the 1880s. As elsewhere, the arrival of the railway greatly increased the town's tourist trade and triggered considerable development of the area.

The town grew out of the village of Torre, which had occupied the site since before the building of the twelfth-century Torre Abbey and the thirteenth-century Spanish Barn – so named because the crew of a Spanish Armada ship was imprisoned there in 1588.

Left: *Anstey's Cove, Torquay, at high tide in 1903. The quiet and secluded cove lies to the north-east of the town.*

Left: *Cockington Sands, seen on a postcard from 1902. This quiet stretch of sand on the southern edge of Torquay offers a sharp contrast to the bustle and crowds of the beaches to the north-east – Babbacombe, Oddicombe and Redgate. Just out of shot, however, Cockington had its bathing machines as well.*

Cockington village, now on the outskirts of Torquay but once separated by a few miles of countryside from the south-west of the town, was a remote hamlet made up of a delightful group of cottages, many thatched and some dating from medieval times. It was visited by many of the town's summer visitors, to whom such sights were completely new. This 1896 view of the village was a popular memento for visitors to take back home with them. Several of the cottages still survive.

Watchet

The small Somerset town of Watchet has never enjoyed much success as a seaside resort, relying instead on a working harbour. These stereoscopic images, dating from 1861, mark an extensive rebuilding of the harbour after a severe storm. Like the view of the group of figures below the Alabaster Cliffs (see page 6), they were the work of local Watchet photographer James Date, who, using the wet collodion process, photographed the rebuilding of the harbour. Ambrotype views are unique – there was no negative from which further copies could be made. Both the images seen here are dated July 1861, at the height of the rebuilding work. The harbour view was taken at low tide to ensure that the ships were grounded – and therefore would not move during the exposure.

Date also took photographs of the building of the West Somerset Railway, also in 1861.

Westcliff-on-Sea

The bandstand, Westcliff-on-Sea, ready for a performance in 1907.

A quiet summer's day on Westcliff-on-Sea's promenade, c.1910, from a postcard view by Valentine of Dundee, with yachts ready to take holiday-makers for a sail, and children paddling in the shallow water below. It is a far cry from the bustle of nearby Southend. Like Francis Frith & Company in Reigate, Valentine's publishing company had produced picture postcards of most British holiday resorts by 1910.

C. Davis was obviously very proud of the bathing machines he rented out at Westcliff, which he roofed with imitation pantiles. Late-Edwardian postcards styled the resort both as 'Westcliff' and as 'Westcliff-on-Sea' – the usual name today – although the resort is now absorbed into Southend-on-Sea.

Weston-super-Mare

A quiet afternoon on the beach, 1908. A telescope on a tripod points out to sea, but nobody is willing to pay to take a look through it!

Weston Sands, 1908.

The quiet shingle beach at Anchor Head, from a 1904 photograph.

The Grand Pier Pavilion, 1907.

The Grand Pier, 1907. The 1000 foot (305 metre) long pier was one of the last of its kind to be built – and opened only four years before this view was taken.

The favourite watering place of a very select few since the end of the eighteenth century, Weston-super-Mare expanded rapidly when the Great Western Railway arrived in 1841. Most of the town's finest buildings date from the second half of the nineteenth century. Eugenius Birch's Birnbeck Pier – the town's first – opened in 1867, to be followed thirty-six years later by the sinking of the piles for the Grand Pier. The Birnbeck Pier, unusually, straddles an island in its 1100 foot (335 metre) length. As the sea withdrew almost that far with each tide even in Victorian times, the length of both piers was the bare minimum necessary to ensure that steamers could tie up at any stage of the tide. The Grand Pier, opened in 1904, had the finest position, dominating the sea front and the bay, and has enjoyed continued popularity into the twenty-first century. By the time the pier opened, the town was enjoying a huge influx of visitors, justifying the expense of such an ambitious project. The Grand Pier was a very late addition to the English seashore, with only three new piers having been built after it – at Felixstowe (1905), Fleetwood (1910) and Deal (1957).

Weymouth

The sight of the train slowly making its way through the town towards the ferry terminal was a feature of a Weymouth holiday until surprisingly recently. The view, taken in about 1908, shows the train having just unloaded a group of passengers embarking on the 98 mile (158 km) crossing on the Jersey steamer. The so-called Weymouth Quay Tramway ran from Weymouth Town station to the Quay station. The wooden-bodied clerestory coaches were a typical feature of railway rolling stock at this time. Being relatively short in length, they could deal adequately with the tight curves on the track as it made its way through the streets. Later rolling stock, with longer coaches, caused a considerable challenge, and for many years the trains had special carriages to overcome the problem – and even then with couplings slackened!

Weymouth Esplanade in 1904. The esplanade was considered to be Weymouth's crowning glory, stretching over half a mile along the edge of the bay. The sender of this card, having recently arrived on the boat from Jersey for a short visit, writes of an excellent lunch at 'The Cosy', and looks forward to repeating his 'glorious voyage' on the steamer.

Brunswick Terrace, Weymouth, was completed in 1827. On the back of this card – sent in 1910 from one holiday-maker to a friend who had returned home to Worcester – the writer refers to forthcoming events such as yacht racing and a military tattoo on the cliffs.

This view of the crowded beach was taken c.1908 and includes a splendid view of the (presumably cheaper) alternative to the individual bathing machine. The 'Ladies Saloon' to the left of the traditional bathing machines could accommodate eight bathers at a time, which – thanks to the very gentle slope of the beach – would not place too much stress on the horses!

Whitley Bay

Whitley Sands, seen here in 1910. Only one bathing machine is in use, at the water's edge.

There were grandiose plans in the nineteenth century to build a fine pier at Whitley Bay to rival the finest, further south in Yorkshire. The plans, however, never got further than the drawing board. Along with Cullercoats and Tynemouth, the town offered the nearest good stretches of beach to Newcastle upon Tyne and was a highly popular destination for summer days out.

Muir Gardens, Whitley Bay, a quiet strip of green between town and sea, seen here in a 1909 postcard view, offered views over the rocky shoreline at the south end of Whitley Sands.

Worthing

Worthing bandstand on a busy summer's day in 1908, with the pier beyond. The pier was completed in 1862 and had been widened about twenty years before this picture was taken – at which time the splendid pavilion at the pierhead (hidden behind the bandstand in this view) – had been completed.

This view of the Worthing beach looking west was published as a postcard in the summer of 1903.

Index